PHOTOGRAPHS BY MARC SEROTA / EDITED BY MARK VANCIL

MARINO

ON THE RECORD

BY DAN MARINO

DESIGNED AND PRODUCED BY

RARE AIR MEDIA
1711 North Paulina, Suite 311, Chicago, Illinois 60622

Library of Congress Card Number: 99-069009
ISBN 1-892866-19-6
Printed in the United States of America
10 9 8 7 6 5 4 3 2 1

This pictorial autobiography is dedicated to my family, friends, and the fans who have supported me throughout my career.

Without the loving support of my mother and father, I wouldn't be able to enjoy the successes of raising a family and playing in the National Football League. My parents created the foundation and set the examples that have made me and my sisters the people we are today.

Sharing my Life and my accomplishments with my wife, Claire, and my children—Alexandria, Daniel, Michael, and Joey, magnifies the joy and happiness I experience every day.

To all the guys I've played ball with and for, from St. Regis grade school and Central Catholic High School to the University of Pittsburgh and the pros...thanks!

13

CONTENTS

I ALWAYS THOUGHT I'D HAVE THE OPPORTUNITY TO PLAY PROFESSIONAL FOOTBALL. FROM THE TIME I WAS TEN OR ELEVEN YEARS OLD I KNEW I'D GET THAT CHANCE.

I

IN THE BEGINNING

SAINT REGIS SCHOOL
PITTSBURGH PA
FOOTBALL TEAM
1971

I think the neighborhood I was raised in had something to do with the development of my athletic skills. I grew up in the Oakland section of Pittsburgh, a very ethnic, working-class neighborhood. The fathers were all hard workers. Some of them punched in at the steel mill just down the parkway, others drove trucks or worked with their hands.

We lived in a kind of row house that was just a couple of blocks from the house my father lived in as a kid. I was older than my two sisters, but in that neighborhood I was one of the youngest boys. As a result, I grew up playing with older guys. The quarterback at Central Catholic High School lived across the street. In pickup games around the neighborhood he would be the quarterback of one team and I would quarterback the other.

I could always throw the ball, so there really was never much question about what position I'd play even though everyone else was two or three years older. And the games were really competitive. You either developed a little bit of toughness or you didn't last. You played to win.

Most of the time we played on a field around the corner from our house. I practically grew up on that field. That's where our St. Regis team practiced. And on weekend nights we'd all go down there to watch sandlot football games.

My dad helped coach the team from our area, so I was one of the water boys. They played against different neighborhoods in full pads, helmets—all the gear. They were just a bunch of good guys who would show up and play hard. But to me, they were football players.

Sometimes it doesn't seem that long ago. I can still remember all the names and most of the faces from those pickup games. Other times it seems like all that was a hundred years ago. Not too long ago they named that field after me. Dan Marino Field...amazing.

For a young boy who wanted to be an athlete, Oakland was a great place to grow up. The street games were not only rough and competitive, but you played constantly. If it wasn't in the street, then it was down at the field or over the bridge at the park.

We played football in the street like some kids played basketball on the playgrounds. But the street was so narrow, you could only have three or four guys on a team. Telephone poles marked the end zones and the curbs were out of bounds. When you weren't dodging a player from the other team you were trying to avoid a car or one of the city buses.

I was a huge Pittsburgh Steelers fan, just like most of the other kids I knew. We'd meet in the street every Sunday morning before the Steelers game. As soon as the game came on television, we'd run in, watch the first half, and then head back out to the street for a quick game before the third quarter.

We'd also play with guys from other parts of the area. Tackle football with no pads...nothing.

But those kinds of games were played all over Pittsburgh, and you can see the results. No one else from my neighborhood went on to play professionally, but Johnny Unitas was from Mt. Washington across the river. Jim Kelly is from East Brady, which is about forty minutes outside the city. Joe Montana grew up about twenty minutes away. And Beaver Falls, where Joe Namath grew up, is about an hour from Oakland. Jeff Hostetler and I played on the same high school all-star team in a game against the West, and George Blanda was from right around my area too. That's an incredible amount of quarterback talent from one little part of the country.

The neighborhood was a mixture of Italian, Irish, African American, and Polish. We had Italians on one side of our house and a Polish family on the other. The Coyne family, which was Irish and had about five kids, lived two doors down. Mr. Coyne used to sit on the porch and drink Iron City Beer when he came home from the

steel mill. Occasionally he'd come down and play catch with us in the street.

I wouldn't say we were middle class. That would have been stretching it a bit. But I could stand on our porch and touch the house next door. My dad worked a lot of hours, but we still lived week to week. His main job was delivering newspaper bundles for the *Pittsburgh Post-Gazette* on the midnight shift.

Every Friday night he'd pull an accounting book out of this little desk, sit down, and figure out how to get us through the next week. He'd pay all the bills, put twenty or thirty dollars in his pocket for the week ahead, then give my mom money for food. When he finished, we'd all get in the car and go shopping at the Giant Eagle.

That was our life. It wasn't like we went without meals or clothes. We had just enough to get by. But we knew it wasn't any different at the other houses in the neighborhood

My father tried teaching me how to throw knuckleballs when I was growing up. I could never throw a very good knuckler, but Larry Lamonde, a kid on my street, sure could. I used to go to University of Pittsburgh baseball games to watch Larry who later made it to Triple A with the Pirates. His knuckleball actually helped extend his baseball career.

Larry and I pitched together for two years in high school. I was 25-0 and he was something like 26-1. We didn't lose until we got to the state championship game. That's one reason baseball almost became my first professional sport.

The Kansas City Royals drafted me in the fourth round after my senior year in high school. I had just signed to play football for the University of Pittsburgh when the Royals called. That was the first year you could sign a professional contract in baseball without losing your college eligibility in football or basketball. Danny Ainge and I were going to be the first players to take advantage of the new rule. (Danny played basketball at Brigham Young and later signed with the Toronto Blue Jays.)

The Royals projected me to be a third baseman even though I was a pretty good pitcher. In the two times the Kansas City scout came to see me I hit three home runs.

So the plan was to play baseball for Kansas City in the summer, then go back to Pitt in the fall and play football. The Royals offered me $35,000 as a signing bonus. That seemed like a huge amount of money until I found out the other part of the eligibility rule. If I signed the baseball con-tract, then I had to pay my own way through college. And Kansas City wouldn't offer any more money because of the risk of football injury.

Jackie Sherrill, my football coach at Pitt, sat me down and laid it all out. If I signed, then I'd have to pay. I knew my dad didn't have that kind of money, so I would have ended up playing baseball for nothing.

It turned out to be an easy decision. Sometimes I wonder what would have happened if I had given baseball a shot.

SOMETIMES I WONDER WHAT WOULD HAVE HAPPENED IF I HAD GIVEN BASEBALL A SHOT

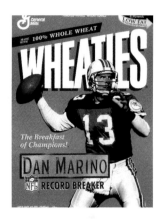
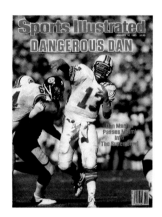

I 've never seen the harm in dreaming big dreams as long as you're willing to work toward them. And I had no problem with that. I thought all along I'd be a professional football player. I think my father knew too. But he always told me, "You don't deserve anything in life. You work for what you deserve."

That's why I was so fortunate to have my dad around when I was young. In a lot of ways I really don't know what I would have done without him. School was a good example. I was so bad early on that my dad finally sat me down and explained the other side of all my dreams. In other words, getting to where I wanted to go involved a lot more than throwing a football well.

He knew I wanted to go to Central Catholic, which was the best school in our neighborhood. That's where you wanted to go if you were at St. Regis. And if you were an athlete, it was the only place. On top of that, we were Catholic, so the idea of choosing a public school wasn't even an option, assuming, of course, you could pass the entrance exams and pay the tuition.

But the way grade school was going I wasn't even going to be able to qualify academically. I remember my dad saying, "If you have these dreams, then you have to get your act in gear so you can get into that high school. Then you have to keep your grades at a certain level so you can get a college scholarship."

I was in sixth grade when we had that discussion. He told me I had to make a decision. Either I had to start concentrating on the books or I wouldn't have a chance.

I think he fueled the fire a little bit by taking me to Central Catholic games. Just sitting in those stands watching the Catholic high school team play made a huge impression. But I also remember

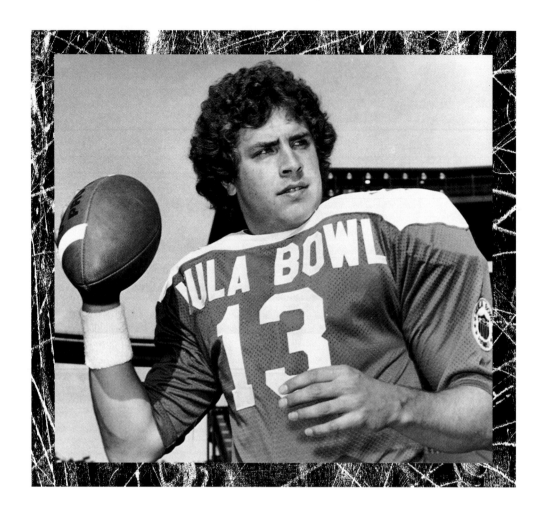

DEEP DOWN PITT WAS WHERE I KNEW I'D END UP.

sitting in school and watching the clock, waiting until I could get out in the street and play ball.

What's amazing is that my dad never said a word about how much it cost to attend Central Catholic. All he cared about was getting the best education for his kids. But I knew we didn't have the money. He'd work weekends with my uncle (he had a small landscaping business) and my mom took a job as a crossing guard at the school. She would get up every morning, no

matter how cold or rainy, fix us breakfast, and head out to the school. She did that for six or seven years to help all three of us get through Central Catholic.

The decision to play football at the University of Pittsburgh after high school really wasn't much different than the decision to attend Central Catholic after grade school. The

PITT WAS WHERE I HAD ALWAYS WANTED TO GO.

main college building was on the same street as Central Catholic and I could see the stadium from my house.

Given my accomplishments in high school, I had the opportunity to play for a number of other schools. But deep down I knew Pitt was where I'd end up. Just the thought of being the starting quarterback for the college team right in your own neighborhood, how many kids get that kind of opportunity? Besides, Pitt had won the national

championship a couple of years earlier and still had a pretty good team.

I visited other schools just to make sure. I went to Michigan State, Notre Dame, UCLA, Arizona State, and Clemson, but I never felt comfortable.

Pitt was where I had always wanted to go. They just seemed flashier with those uniforms and everything. And even though I didn't have a whole lot to do with it, Miami was probably the best place for me to go after my four years at Pitt.

All I have to do is look around to know my kids will never go through the kind of experiences I had back in Pittsburgh. We had the public transportation bus coming past my front door every twenty minutes. There were streetlights, pigeons everywhere, those orange clouds from the steel mill, that awful smell, and not much grass anywhere.

I mean, if I didn't have anything else to do I'd get a football, go out into the street, and throw at telephone poles. I'd move around cars like I was avoiding a pass rush and try to hit a pole. Then I'd pick up the ball and do it again. I had a football, and bat, and glove. I didn't have Nintendo, electric cars, or roller blades. Kids don't even ride bikes anymore. In my neighborhood it was pretty cool just to have a bike.

I've played seventeen seasons in the National Football League and experienced things I couldn't have imagined growing up in Pittsburgh. Every once in a while that reality still hits me. Standing on a stage singing songs with Hootie and the Blowfish, strapping myself into an F-16 fighter jet. I always had big dreams, but in a lot of ways my life has actually turned out better than the dreams.

I'VE EXPERIENCED THING
I COUDN'T HAV

MAGINED
GROWING UP IN PITTSBURGH

JACKIE PULLED ME ASIDE EARLY IN MY FRESHMAN SEASON AND TOLD ME, "THIS IS THE BEST ADVICE I'M EVER GOING TO GIVE YOU. DON'T EVER LET ANYONE TELL YOU HOW TO THROW THE FOOTBALL."

II

THE ROAD TO SUNDAY

Don Shula was a good coach for me early in my career. His teams were disciplined, which was important, especially for a young quarterback trying to learn a pro system.

By the time I arrived in the Dolphins' camp I knew I was good enough to play at that level. I knew I had the arm and was confident I would be able to adapt to all of the other responsibilities.

But what really helped was the way Coach Shula treated me those first couple of years. He forced me to advance quickly by making me call all my own plays almost from the start. Then, just to make sure I was progressing, Shula would put me on the spot with very specific questions about plays, situations, or options.

I wanted to make sure I was right when he tossed out those questions, so I probably studied a lot harder than I might have otherwise. And the more I showed I could handle the load, the more he piled it on. I think he sensed I could handle the pressure, so he just kept pushing harder and harder.

Shula forced me to progress. But I was also fortunate to have a lot of veteran guys around me. Nat Moore, one of our receivers, would help me out in the huddle. If I screwed up the call, Nat would set me straight. But Shula knew how to get me going. He knew how to pinch the right nerve and press the right buttons. And I responded, just as he knew I would, by studying longer and playing harder.

It wasn't until years later that I realized what Shula had done to me those first seasons. He knew exactly what he was doing and exactly how hard to push. But I wasn't the only one Shula tested. That was his way of finding out exactly where people fit.

In my case, particularly early in my career, Shula and I fit well together. He also became a good friend.

I had good solid coaching from the time I was a kid. My dad helped me develop my physical skills at a young age. In terms of pure throwing mechanics, he is probably most responsible.

I mean, God gives you a certain amount of natural ability. But then someone has to help you develop those skills properly. Probably the greatest compliment to my father's coaching ability came from Jackie Sherrill, my coach at Pitt.

Jackie pulled me aside early in my freshman season and told me, "This is the best advice I'm ever going to give you. Don't ever let anyone tell you how to throw the football. Just keep throwing it the way you do. Don't let any coach tell you any different."

IT WASN'T UNTIL YEARS LATER THAT I REALIZED WHAT SHULA HAD DONE TO ME THOSE FIRST COUPLE YEARS

My dad had always taught me to throw without any wasted motion. Even in the house waiting for dinner we'd toss a ball back and forth in the living room. He made me think about little things like mechanics at a very early age.

When I went to my first camp with the Dolphins, Shula took the same position as Jackie. He watched me throw and just let me go.

To some extent, my senior season at Pitt prepared me mentally for what I was about to face in the NFL.

I was one of the favorites to win the Heisman Trophy and we were supposed to have the best team in the country even though you couldn't tell by our record.

We had lost three games in my first three seasons, then we lost three my senior year. As if that wasn't bad enough given the expectations, the NFL was on strike that year. So instead of playing in the shadow of the Steelers, everyone focused on what was happening in college football.

It wasn't like I played that badly, but it turned into an extremely difficult year. We all thought the preseason hype was on target. But we just didn't get the job done. For the first time in my athletic career, disappointment and frustration were directed at me, the leader and, most important, the quarterback.

In a strange way, that whole experience made my transition to professional football a little easier. I think it taught me, among other things, how to deal with the media. I went from being the Associated Press All-American quarterback to not even making the All East College football team.

But, in the end, everything that happened made me a little tougher mentally.

I took a lot of things for granted before I got hurt in 1993. I sort of forgot how lucky I had been, how blessed my career was up to that point. I don't forget anymore. I can't forget.

The brace I wear around my right ankle is a result of the Achilles tendon I tore in 1993. The Achilles, the first real injury of my career, turned out to be a wake-up call.

I had played in 145 straight games, an NFL record for quarterbacks, when I was knocked to the ground after throwing a pass against Cleveland. The brace I wear on my left knee goes halfway up my thigh and down around my calf. Going into the 1999 season I had had five arthroscopic knee operations—oil changes I like to call them.

I had gone over ten years doing what I love, without really missing any games. And then all of a sudden it was gone, taken away in a single moment. It made me realize how much I appreciate playing and how much I enjoyed the competitive aspect of the game. You walk into a visiting stadium with everybody against you and there's a certain confidence that you can take on everybody and make it happen.

But the time away taught me to savor every second. That's why I have worked harder these last two years than at any time in my career. I even took up yoga as an exercise, something I never would have considered in the past.

But yoga has really helped, especially with flexibility. I have always had arthritis in my knee, but I started doing yoga and now the pain isn't as severe. It's crazy, but it works.

Even during the off-season I have to work those muscles. Any given day I'm either riding a stationary bike, doing squats, leg presses, or a combination of all three.

A bout six years ago, after my eleventh NFL season, I started coming in on postgame Monday mornings for a therapeutic massage. It helps, but the real pain usually doesn't set in until Tuesday or Wednesday. The good news is that the massage, along with the delayed reaction of any pain, allows me to work out and get some blood flowing through my muscles on Monday.

It's especially important because Mondays are the longest days of the week. With Shula, guys came in early to get treatment, then we usually had a film session followed by conditioning drills. We'd also have a quarterbacks meeting later in the afternoon.

The idea is to get a good first look at the team we were playing the next week. You want to get a feel for their personnel, who's playing where, what they do on their specialty coverages.

For me, Mondays usually start about 10 A.M. and last into the early evening. We always take Tuesday off, but depending upon how I feel I try to come in for another workout.

Once Wednesday rolls around we start focusing on the team ahead. With Shula, that would be the day the offense would start putting in the game plan.

We go over the other team's statistical tendencies. What kind of defense do they play on third and long, an obvious passing situation? Then you get into watching films, and that's when the week starts getting interesting to me. We review the run offense. I have to know not only the plays we think we'll use, but alternate plays I can call at the line of scrimmage if the defense changes.

We used to do a lot of what we called "check with me," which meant I would call the play in the huddle, but no one knew which direction it would go until I got up to the line and figured out the defensive front.

By Thursday, the offensive coordinator, the Dolphins backup quarterback Bernie Kosar, and myself go over third-down calls we think we might run against this particular team. We might narrow one hundred plays down to fifteen. But if at any time it looks like something else might work, I have the option of going back to the other eighty-five plays.

By the end of the week I've compiled my own little game plan. I'll have a list of plays after talking with the offensive coordinator and the offensive line coach. Then I write down the eight best running plays.

I'll also have first-down passing plays broken down by formation. And I'll write out the entire call, something like "Fly to Red Right, 94." Eventually I will have an entire play list broken down by formation. Then I make sixteen copies and pass them out to all the backs, receivers, and quarterbacks.

I'm not sure how many quarterbacks do this during the week, but I like to run drills in practice to stay sharp and comfortable with the defensive pass rush.

When our defense is practicing against the "scout team," which runs the opponent's plays, I'll step in and be the quarterback. I want to maintain that feel for the rush.

JIMMY GETS RIGHT TO THE POINT. I RESPECT THAT.

From what I've seen from Jimmy Johnson, we're a lot alike. He's very involved in what his players are doing and committed to doing whatever it takes to win. Even during the off-season he spent time in the weight room watching players work out.

He told us how things were going to be run and what he wanted to accomplish. Jimmy gets right to the point. I respect that.

He said he was going to treat everybody differently. He came right out and said, "The guys that work their butts off and show me they're good players, I'm going to treat them great. Other guys that might not be great players but work their butts off and perform for me and believe in what I'm doing, I'm going to treat them great too. But then there are the great players that don't work and don't practice. I'm going to treat you like garbage."

I remember early on when Jimmy was asked whether he was trying to win a Super Bowl for Dan Marino. His answer: He's trying to win a ring for himself. And that's fine with me because I feel the same way. As a player, you're trying to win a Super Bowl for yourself within the team concept. It's no different for the coaches.

I know he wouldn't have taken the job if he didn't think we could win quickly. It's not like he walked into a situation like the one he inherited in Dallas. We have some very talented people.

Just like he said in one of the first meetings, "If you believe in what I'm doing, we're going to win a Super Bowl. A lot of you are going to be here with me, but a lot of you aren't."

I like that. If I was coaching, I'm pretty sure that's exactly how I'd approach things.

MY GOAL IS THE SAME EVERY YEAR: WIN THE SUPER BOWL. IT'S THAT SIMPLE.

III

GAME FACE

The last twenty-four to thirty-six hours leading up to the game is when you really hone in and sharpen your focus.

If we're playing at home I'll go over the notes on Saturday and try to get a mental image of each play. I try to visualize every moment, from calling the play in the huddle to walking up to the line and looking over the defense. I go through everything I have to know, as well as everything everyone else has to know.

Then I review all my options, the blocking assignments, where the ball will be delivered if it's a pass, or what side I'll hand off if it's a running play. I try to visualize the entire process from start to finish. I've always done that. And I've always been able to create a mental image of what's going to happen in the game.

I've heard about other athletes trying to use visualization to help their performance. For me, it's something that's always been a very natural part of my preparation.

In a lot of ways, the coaching change was an even bigger deal to me because I had played for one coach my entire professional career. I'll never forget what Don Shula and I went through for thirteen seasons. He helped me become the player I am today, and hopefully I contributed to his career as well.

But that's the only environment I'd known as a professional. For all the players that came and went during those years, Shula and I were constants. Eventually I knew exactly what he was thinking, what he might say in a given situation or how he would react. I'm sure he felt like he knew me just as well.

So I was probably more anxious and excited leading up to the 1996 season than I had been for a long time. I didn't necessarily know what to expect. And for the first time in my pro career I had somebody else critiquing my performance.

I think my career speaks for itself, but I liked the idea of having to prove myself again. It's all so fresh. I've played for seventeen years, but I look at the time I have left as a new, though shorter, career.

I want to win a Super Bowl. But at this point, I don't think failing to win one is going to take away from what I have accomplished on the football field. You gain a certain respect for consistency, work ethic, and whatever you are able to accomplish because of those things.

One of my college roommates was Tommy Flynn. Ever heard of him? He was a safety at Pitt chosen in the fourth round by the Green Bay Packers. He played two years in Green Bay, was waived, and then got picked up by the New York Giants. He played special teams for the Giants the year New York won the Super Bowl. The next year he plays half a season and is out of the game. But he's got a Super Bowl ring.

I WANT TO WIN A SUPERBOWL. BUT AT THIS POINT, I DON'T THINK FAILING TO WIN ONE IS GOING TO TAKE AWAY FROM WHAT I'VE ACCOMPLISHED ON THE FOOTBALL FIELD.

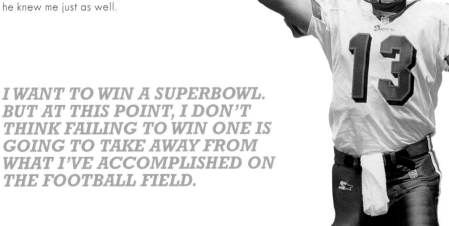

You have to be with the right people in the right situation at the right time. And sometimes you need some luck. One thing I do have in my favor is that the way the NFL is set up now, the league is much more wide-open. There are no dynasties.

We're not that much different than anyone else It's not like the years when San Francisco was winning, or even when Jimmy Johnson was in Dallas.

It's getting the right people, applying the right philosophy, and having enough star players who can make things happen. You can find the other players, and the right system can help them raise their level of play. That's what we have to do. I really don't think we're that far away.

Confidence comes through experience. Still, there's always some level of doubt the closer you get to Sunday. It's just a slight apprehension really. When you get to this level, for me anyway, there's that pressure of knowing I have to perform week in and week out.

I know I have to play well in order for us all to do well. I don't want to sound cocky or arrogant, but that's the way it's been, particularly the last few years.

I think it's natural and good that I'm still apprehensive. It's important to get the adrenaline flowing. You need to feel that the game is important to you. Lose that feeling and you lose your edge. There's no faking that kind of emotion. You can't invent the feeling. It's got to be natural, real.

Football is different than any of the other team sports because so much rides on each regular season game. In basketball, baseball, or hockey, a loss is just one of 80 to 162 games, depending on the sport. We play sixteen times during the regular season.

Even the play-offs are dramatically different. You play once for the AFC championship, once for the Super Bowl, winner take all. That's what makes it so unique, especially with the position I play. Quarterback is probably the hardest individual position in all of team sports.

> *FOOTBALL IS DIFFERENT THAN ANY OF THE OTHER TEAM SPORTS BECAUSE SO MUCH RIDES ON EACH REGULAR SEASON GAME.*

Some people have tried to compare playing quarterback to being a goalie in hockey. But goalies really don't have to think. They have to anticipate and react to stop shots, but they don't have to break down a defense at the line of scrimmage, change a play, and remember not only what everyone on their team is supposed to do but what the opponent is likely to do. And then, in three to four seconds, drop back, pick out a receiver, and put the ball in the air.

Everything becomes a little more real on Saturday morning. We'll come in and do more film work, then have a walk-through, which is a physical review of what we're going to do on both sides of the ball.

That night, if it's a home game, we'll have a quarterback meeting at 8 o'clock or so and just talk. That's one place Bernie Kosar was really valuable. He came up with good questions. He also was able to point out things the rest of us might have missed. For years I didn't have anyone like that.

But like a lot of my teammates over the years, there was one other side of Bernie I had to get used to. Because we worked so closely together, Shula wanted us to room together the night before games. So the first night Bernie hands me a pair of earplugs. I said, "What are these for?" He says, "Just use them. You'll need 'em."

I've never heard anybody snore as loud as Bernie. It didn't take long until we decided to get a suite with separate bedrooms.

SOME PEOPLE HAVE TRIED TO COMPARE QUARTERBACK TO BEING A GOALIE IN HOCKEY

We always stay at a team hotel, even when the game is in Miami. The idea is to eliminate distractions so you can concentrate on the game and hopefully get a good night's sleep. I used to stay at home from time to time, but I don't anymore. With all my kids, one of them is usually up sometime in the middle of the night and I need to get my rest.

But it's only been during the last few years that I've been able to get in a full night of sleep before a game, regardless of where I stayed. I remember nights when I'd sit straight up in bed, wide awake because I'd be thinking, or dreaming, "Here comes a strong safety blitz." For the most part I've gotten past those kinds of nights. But every once in a while I'll see somebody coming.

I REMEMBER NIGHTS WHEN I'D SIT STRAIGHT UP IN BED, WIDE AWAKE BECAUSE I'D BE THINKING, OR DREAMING, "HERE COMES A STRONG SAFETY BLITZ."

BY SUNDAY I'M NOT THE SAME GUY I WAS ON WEDNESDAY.

IV

SUNDAY

By the time I run onto the field I'm totally tuned into the game. I've had people tell me they've said hello and I just looked right through them. It's like I don't see anything outside of the game once I'm on the field.

You'd think you were talking to two different people if you saw me early in the week, then minutes before a game. By Sunday I'm not the same guy I was on Wednesday. In a way I'm not the same person. It's a slow transformation that builds toward kick-off.

My routine is pretty much the same on Sunday. I just sit in the trainer's room, read over my notes, and listen to the guys as they come in. The television is usually on with one of the pregame shows, but that's off in the distance.

Sometimes I fall asleep for a little while. But everyone is different. Some guys don't show up until an hour before the game. They'll get taped, dressed, and go. One thing I don't do is talk a whole lot before the game. Because you do it so often, most players end up with some kind of ritual for getting taped and then dressed for a game.

It's not like I try to follow the same exact move down to the smallest details, but the one thing I do is have someone help me put my jersey on before the game. My first six years it was always Don Strock, the Dolphins' backup quarterback. I had Jim Jensen for a while. Then, for about three years, I didn't let anyone do it. When Bernie Kosar arrived, I turned the job over to him.

And I always used to shake Shula's hand before the game. Right before the kickoff, when he brings everyone up and the special teams leave, I'd go up and say, "Have a good game." I'd do that before every game. That was definitely a habit. But, I've never really had any superstitions like making sure I put my left knee pad in before my right.

A few years ago, Irving Fryar, who's an ordained minister, would do a prayer. I went to the Catholic Mass, so I didn't feel like I needed to go to Irving's prayer. But he'd still come over and bless me on the forehead with holy water. I always thought, "Hey, if that stuff works, go ahead, put in on my knee, my arm, everywhere."

There's a certain confidence, almost a feeling, that you can take on that entire stadium and make something happen for your team. It's that "me against the world" adrenaline rush you get when you walk into a stadium on the road.

I get that feeling going into Buffalo, which is one of the toughest places to play, or New York. I look out and think, "I'm the quarterback and I'm going to come in here today with these forty-four other guys and beat your team." You can feel the hostility and you know just about everyone in that place is against you. But there's something about that moment when you walk out onto the field and into the fire that gets me going.

I think it's especially true in my position, because I have to deal with the crowd. You can't imagine what it feels like to do something that silences almost eighty thousand people.

A good example is the time I faked a spike against the New York Jets. The entire stadium was going crazy because they thought they had held us off. They were up by twenty-six points and it was going to be their first division title in I don't know how many years. But in the second half I threw four touchdowns and we got right back into the game.

Then we got the ball back with about a minute to play and I remember thinking, "We've got a shot. We're going to win this game." The crowd's going crazy, all seventy-eight thousand of them.

So we get down near the goal line and time's running out. I take the snap and everyone thinks I'm going to spike the ball to stop the clock. But Bernie Kosar and I had practiced faking the spike. We were just waiting for the right opportunity to use it in a game. No one could have expected us to pull it off in that situation. It was second down and we were on the eight-yard line. We needed three points to tie.

But I knew I had the field goal in my pocket, so I thought, "This is the perfect time for the clock play." I walked up to the line, took the snap, and took one step back. I looked down and faked a throw into the dirt, which was exactly what everybody in the place expected, including the Jets. Then I looked over and found Irving for the touchdown.

The place went silent. I looked up and thought, "Where are all you people now?" That's a great feeling. Me against the world.

YOU HEAR THE CROWD PARTICULARLY AT BUFFALO

IF IT'S THIRD AND ONE AND AN IMPORTANT PART OF THE GAME, MY GUYS CAN HARDLY HEAR ME CALL THE PLAY, AND THAT'S IN THE HUDDLE.

YOU WOULDN'T BE HUMAN IF YOU DIDN'T THINK ABOUT...

GETTING.

Y ou wouldn't be human if you didn't think about getting hurt. That reality is always somewhere in the back of your mind. But I have enough confidence in my knowledge of the game to feel relatively safe within the parameters of my position.

But freak things happen, like knocking a finger out of joint by hitting a helmet or tearing knee cartilage. And even though you're used to the violence, there are certain hits where you kind of say to yourself, "Damn, did he get hit hard."

So you do think about it. But you don't focus on what can happen. You can't. Once the adrenaline starts flowing and you get into the excitement of the game, the reality, or possibility, of being hurt leaves your mind.

When you do take a particularly hard hit, like the one Gregg Lloyd laid on me in a game against Pittsburgh, you really don't feel anything on the initial contact. On that play, my natural reaction was to jump up because I was mad. I thought it was a late hit. I wanted to grab

HURT

him, get in his face, and let him know exactly how I felt. And that's what I was going to do until I realized I couldn't breathe. I couldn't even get a word out. I remember thinking, "Just lay back down."

I was kind of spinning a little bit, my arm hurt, my wind was gone. You eventually feel the pain, but still not to the extent you do a day or two later. Your body is loose, the adrenaline is pumping, and you're into the game mentally and physically. So the pain really is a secondary condition, something that doesn't quite find its way into your mind until all the other elements have disappeared.

I've always had a knack for knowing where defensive players are when I'm in the pocket. I might not see them, but I've always been able to feel their presence. That's helped me avoid taking the kinds of big shots I've seen other quarterbacks take.

I can look and have somebody coming right at me and without ever looking directly at them I can stay focused downfield and just step out of the way as they go by. All the while I'm still focused on where I'm going to throw the ball. That's something you can't teach. And it's something I've always been able to do. In that three- or four-yard area in the pocket, I've always been quick enough or aware enough to move away from trouble and still keep my body in position to throw with velocity and accuracy. I think that's one of my best attributes as a quarterback.

There are times when I feel so comfortable that guys can be coming at me and I just calmly move away from them and make the throw. It's not like anything is in slow motion, but there is a rhythm and I'm completely in sync.

I'm not sure where it came from, although I did jump rope a lot when I was younger. I've never been fast, but I've always had pretty quick feet and good footwork.

There probably isn't as much give-and-take in the huddle as people might think. A lot of times I don't feel like I'm getting enough feedback from my receivers. I'll try to remind them, "If you feel certain things can work, then I want you to tell me."

If we're running the ball, I usually ask the linemen what it looks like from their perspective. What's your favorite running play right now? What do you think will work? That doesn't mean I'll do it, but I like the input.

I've done that a lot the last three or four years because we've had so much change. When you're playing with guys that have been around you for six or seven years, like Mark Clayton and Mark Duper, they know what to do. I didn't have to say much to them.

But other times I'll take matters into my own hands. I remember a game against the Rams when they were still in Los Angeles. They had Jim Everett at quarterback and Eric Dickerson in the backfield. Before you knew it they went up by something like twenty-one points.

At that point I walked up to every offensive player on our team and I said, "We're not running the ball again until we get ahead." Shula was calling the plays, but I told them, "I don't care

THERE PROBABLY ISN'T AS MUCH GIVE-AND-TAKE IN THE HUDDLE AS PEOPLE MIGHT THINK.

what he calls. We're throwing every pass from now until we get the lead."

Shula would send in a running play and I'd call a pass. I didn't even bother calling the play he had sent in. I called it right there in the huddle. We were throwing the ball and that was that. When Duper and Clayton heard that, it just took those guys to a different level. That's all they wanted to hear. The ball's going in the air.

But to Shula's credit, he always gave me that option.

I ended up throwing five touchdowns and we won in overtime on a touchdown pass to Duper.

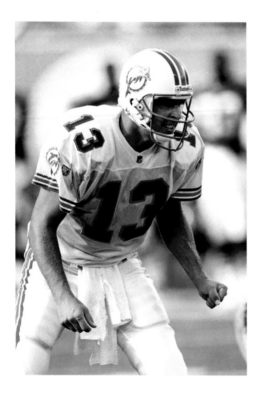

When I look downfield I see everything by areas. I see what the receiver is doing, which way the defensive back is moving, whether there are any other receivers or defensive players in that zone, as well as what's happening all around me.

But when it's time to get rid of the ball I focus in and throw. It's like I'm looking at an entire picture of whatever play we're running, not just one guy.

Some games stand out more than others. I remember one against the Steelers in the Orange Bowl, when they still had Donnie Shell and Jack Lambert. That game shot us toward Super Bowl XIX.

I remember a lot about that game because I grew up a Steelers fan and the game meant so much. The score ended up 45-28 and I had 4 touchdowns and 421 yards passing. We all had a good game that day.

Another one that stands out is the game against Oakland when I broke the single-season touchdown record. That's when the Raiders still had a great defense. That game was in the Orange Bowl too, and it turned into a shootout. We had Clayton and Duper and they had Mike Haynes and Lester Hayes at the corners. Lyle Alzedo was still playing and so was Howie Long. We ended up losing 48-45, but it was such a great football game.

I always remember the games when we came back from behind. Those are two of them, but there has been a lot over the years. Some of the Jets games were fun, especially in the Meadowlands. I remember the game when I threw four touchdowns in the second half to bring us back, all of them to Mark Ingram. That was kind of neat, especially when you silence seventy-thousand New York fans.

here are two ways of looking at fourth quarter pressure situations. If we're behind and have to make something happen offensively, it can turn into a street ball game. I start calling plays, changing them at the line, and suddenly everything becomes a little more chaotic. Players on both sides of the ball are hustling into position on every play. You're trying to make them adjust; they're trying to make us adjust. And everything is happening more quickly and with less organization than earlier in the game. It often comes down to which team can improvise and make plays.

I was able to do that a couple of times early in my career. I pulled out a game or two under those circumstances. Once you've done it you know you can do it again. The fear factor is gone. After a while you know you can make it happen in the last minute or two of a game.

When your confidence gets to that point, you even start looking forward to those moments. It's almost as if I become more comfortable, more focused. I like the challenge. I start calling plays on the basis of what feels right. To a certain extent I

know what kind of defense they're going to play and how to exploit it.

I know, for example, there are going to be times within the last two minutes of a game when the defense is going to take a chance too. So if I catch them at the right time, one play can end the game. I wait for that moment and if it happens, I try to take advantage. But while I'm looking for that one shot, I know I have to keep moving the team downfield to get into field goal position.

The fourth-quarter huddle is a little different than at other times during the game, but not as much as you might think. Players concentrate more and focus on what I'm saying because everything has to be communicated so much more quickly.

To be honest, as much as I might relish that situation when it presents itself, I'd rather be running the clock out and nailing down a victory. Even though John Elway, Joe Montana, and I have been good at making things happen to win games in the final moments, if you ask them they'll tell you running down the clock to preserve a victory is a lot better than having the clock run down while you're trying to find a victory.

good example of what can happen to a player, mentally as well as physically, was what happened to me in Miami versus Indianapolis in 1995. I tore the cartilage in my right knee in the second quarter. But instead of coming out of the game, I just told the trainer what had happened. I'd torn knee cartilage before so I was confident I had made the right diagnosis.

He asked me what I wanted to do and I said, "Well, I think I can play. It's just clicking a little bit when I run." Once it's torn, it's torn, so I figured I'd just play until I couldn't go anymore. Then I got hit real hard, a direct shot on my right hip. Again, I felt the pain, but it really didn't hinder me as much as it should have because I was so mentally and physically into the game.

Then, about the fourth quarter, I felt a burning sensation around the hip. As the pain intensified I completely forgot about my knee. In fact, my knee really didn't hurt at all.

After the game, doctors confirmed the torn cartilage and scheduled surgery for the next morning. To them, the hip wasn't that big of a deal. But it continued to burn and swell. Then, at about five in the morning, I woke up in a cold sweat. I looked at my hip and it had swollen to the size of a basketball. The fluid, or blood, had built up around my hip and upper thigh to the point that I felt like I was going to pass out.

I told Claire to get me to the hospital right away. I was supposed to be there at 9 A.M. anyway for the knee surgery, so when I arrived they hooked me up to an IV and gave me something for the pain.

A little while later, after taking care of the hip, they did my knee. I always try to stay awake for knee operations for a couple of reasons. First, I want to watch the process. Second, I've been put to sleep for various surgeries and for me, coming out of the anesthesia is worse than the surgery itself. But after they did my knee they decided to drain all the blood out of my hip. It ended up bleeding for ten days.

It bled so much that my blood count actually dropped. So every four hours around the clock I had to change all the dressings. This was right in the middle of the season. Meanwhile, my knee was fine. To this day there is a strange sensation around that area of my hip because all the nerve endings were damaged.

The point is, I missed one series in that game against the Colts. Even with a serious hip contusion and torn knee cartilage, the intensity and emotion of a game is enough to eliminate, or at lease diminish, a lot of pain.

But later on, after you've left the game and the game has left you, the pain is real. I've been hurt before, broken ribs and things like that, but I don't think I've ever had as much pain as I did with that hip.

In fact, during that first week after the Colts game, when it hurt so bad I could hardly sleep and the blood was everywhere, I wondered whether after thirteen years the game was worth all this. I really started to question myself and just how much longer I could pay the price.

But, like the pain, that eventually passed.

IT HURT SO BAD I COULD HARDLY SLEEP AND THE BLOOD WAS EVERYWHERE, I WONDERED WHETHER AFTER THIRTEEN YEARS THE GAME WAS WORTH ALL THIS.

There are times on the field when I feel like I can't miss, when I'm in complete control and everything just clicks. The ball is always on time, it's always catchable, and I'm making the right decisions on who to throw to. Those are the times when I want to pass on every play because I feel like we're unstoppable. It's almost like I slip into a groove.

But to set the kinds of records I did during the 1995 season, a combination of factors had to go right. And for us, they did. Over the years, our key personnel has stayed healthy. We have had great receivers. And the protection has been excellent, both from the offensive linemen and the running backs.

the passing-attempts record Sunday, so they're going to stop the game."

Then he'd talk about what I had accomplished. It did make me feel a little uncomfortable, but I knew he felt good about what was happening. He knew he was a part of those records, too, because we were the longest-running combination of quarterback and coach in football history.

We had a special relationship. We had been through a lot together and it made me feel good that he had so much respect for what I was doing on the field. I was injured when he broke the record for coaching victories, but he came into the locker room and thanked me for what I had done to help him get that record. I had more wins

WE HAD A SPECIAL RELATIONSHIP

Finally, to even come close to breaking passing records, you have to throw the ball a lot. Since what we do best is throw the ball, and we have thrown more often than anyone else, I have been in the position to break some records. I'll admit that I have been absolutely thrilled to be a part of it all. The records are something I am very proud of and will never forget. And I won't lie, I have enjoyed the praise and respect that has come my way.

To know you've done something no one else has done is special, particularly when you have twenty-five career records instead of one or two. Shula also made the records hard to ignore. I knew they were important to him and that meant a lot to me. In team meetings he would come right out and say, "We all know Dan's going to break

as a quarterback for Shula than Bob Griese or any of the other guys he's had did.

But neither of us were ever hung up on personal statistics. The only stat I have ever really been concerned about is the number of victories we have at the end of the year. To me, consistency is the key to being a great player. And great players help their teams win games. Like I've said before, my goal each and every year has always been the same: to win the Super Bowl. It's that simple.

In the final analysis, none of us, particularly quarterbacks, are measured by individual accomplishments. By lining up each and every week, with or without aches and pains, my teammates know I am out there to help us win. And players are measured by how much they win.

Dan is congratulated by Don Shula after he broke Fran Tarkenton's touchdown passing record with his 343rd career touchdown pass in Indianapolis on November 26, 1995.

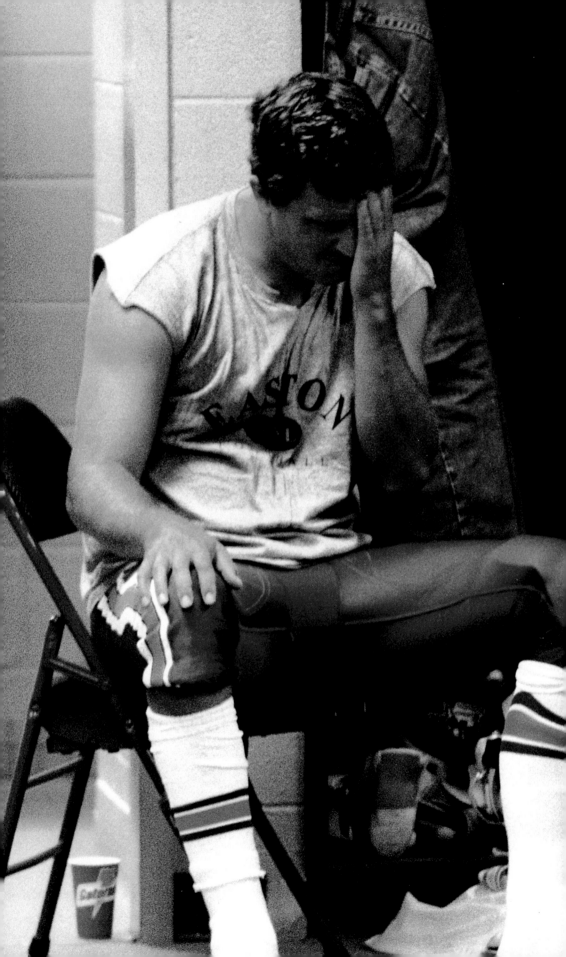

The impact of whatever happened on the field doesn't really set in until the rush of the game wears off and you're sitting in the locker room. If it's been a particularly painful afternoon I might take some mild anti-inflammatory medication right after the game to keep the inflammation down in my knees or the swelling out of the joints in my arm, ankles, or wherever else I might need relief.

Not only does it take the edge off the aches and pains, but it allows me to get a good workout in on Monday, before the real pain sets in.

Overall, I think I've had a good relationship with the media. It's really a matter of accepting the fact that they have a job to do, too. I have an obligation, given my position on the team, to cooperate and, if I can, take the heat off some of the other guys.

I pay attention, but I don't read everything that's written. But everyone's sensitive to what's said or written about them. I know I am.

Not many reporters have experienced what goes on during the course of a season or even during an individual game. So they just aren't going to understand some of the subtleties. Something that seems like a big deal when it hap-

I THINK CLAIRE UNDERSTANDS THE DEMANDS I HAVE AS A PROFESSIONAL FOOTBALL PLAYER.

pens maybe doesn't mean anything in the larger picture. Or maybe there are other explanations for what happened. The players and the coaches know, but it's probably unreasonable to expect somebody sitting in the press box to see everything happening and then figure out the reasons for the results. A lot of times the explanation is really much simpler than it's made out to be.

I think Claire understands the demands I have as a professional football player, but I know my kids don't have any idea about the mental and physical aspects of my job. Even Claire, as close as she is to the day-to-day experience, can only grasp so much.

The only way anyone could really understand is if they went through it themselves. As for the kids, they see me coming home after operations, or with my hip swollen and bleeding, and they know what I do is a little different from the jobs of other dads. It really doesn't seem to scare them. Their response is usually more along the lines of, "I'm never going to play football like Dad." Some days I can't blame them.

At the same time, I've never done their job either. So the give-and-take is exactly that. For the most part we're all just trying to do the best we can within the context of our respective jobs. And I don't have any problem with that.

MY PARENTS WOULD ALWAYS SAY, "IT DOESN'T MATTER IF IT'S A GUY PICKING UP THE GARBAGE OR THE PRESIDENT OF THE UNITED STATES, TREAT EVERYBODY AS YOU WOULD WANT TO BE TREATED."

V

GOING HOME AGAIN

My kids are wonderful. When Claire and I were married we never really talked about how many children we would have. Then, before you knew it, we had four. And they're great, they really are. I wouldn't have it any other way.

Sometimes I wonder how I am as a father to my children compared to how my father was with us. But the circumstances are so different. His lifestyle wasn't even close to mine. And any pressure I might experience really isn't anything like the kind of pressure my father had when we were kids. He was worried about feeding his family. I worry about taking care of my family, but I really don't have to worry about whether or not we're going to be able to eat next week.

SOMETIMES I WONDER HOW I AM AS A FATHER TO MY CHILDREN COMPARED TO HOW MY FATHER WAS WITH US.

I suppose there was a time when I had to worry about whether I'd have a job, but not anymore. That's another thing my father always had to think about. It's hard to even comprehend that kind of pressure because it's something I'll probably never know.

Then I look at my kids. They're into sports a little bit, but nothing like I was at their age. They just have so much more available to them. I mean, we take them to Vail to go skiing. Are you kidding me? That kind of thing didn't even enter my mind until five or six years ago. Even in college or during my first couple of years as a pro, I never thought of taking vacations to places like that. Now these guys go on trips two or three times a year.

But Claire and I try to impart the same values, the idea of being a good person and treating others as you want to be treated. My parents would always say, "It doesn't matter if it's a guy picking up the garbage or the President of the United States, treat everybody as you would want to be treated."

I think that kind of respect is a product of the kind of person you are, how you were raised, where you went to school—all those things.

I realize my children don't completely understand what I do or what all the records mean. But I know they will someday. That's why I wanted to make sure my family, including my children, was in Indianapolis when I broke Fran Tarkenton's record for touchdown passes.

I also love the fact that my mother and father are able to enjoy what I'm doing.

I REALLY DO BELIEVE IN TRYING TO GIVE SOMETHING BACK TO THE COMMUNITY

My parents always seemed to know how to say the right thing at the right time. My father was that way when it came to me playing sports. Sometimes I wonder if I'll have that ability. Where does that knowledge or wisdom come from? He would always know how to tie an athletic situation back into life and at the time, it seemed like it always was exactly what I needed to hear.

That kind of perspective is just about impossible to recognize or figure out on your own. But I had my mom and dad there. My mother is one of the most amazing people I have ever known. She possesses a warmth and strength that I appreciate even more as I grow older. It was an incredible experience having both of them around my life as a child. Still is.

As a professional athlete I am judged not only by what I do on the field, but by what I contribute off the field. I know responsibility comes with the celebrity or status that we enjoy from playing at this level.

I'm sure it has something to do with the way I was raised or the place I came from, but I really do believe in trying to give something back to the community after all the community has done for me and my family. It's a very small price to pay compared to how fortunate I have been in my life.

I KNOW HOW IMPORTANT IT IS TO SPEND TIME WITH MY WIFE AND CHILDREN BECAUSE I KNOW WHAT IT MEANT TO ME TO HAVE MY FATHER AND MOTHER AROUND WHEN I WAS GROWING UP.

I know how important it is to spend time with my wife and children because I know what it meant to me to have my father and mother around when I was growing up. During the season, that's not always easy. Between practices, meetings, appearances, and other football-related responsibilities, the hours can disappear quickly. But I need that balance and I know that my kids and my wife need it as well.

Having a family of my own has taught me about life. When Claire and I found out that Michael, our second oldest, was autistic, it changed our lives. When everything is going fine and great you have a tendency to miss some of the things that are happening to others. But Michael has helped me understand more about life and what's important. I know that what he's doing is a lot harder than anything I have to do on a football field. And yet he goes along without complaint. Our experience with Michael has put things in perspective.

I know we're very lucky. Michael is a beautiful kid, a loving kid, and very social. He is not a severe case. And he's got two brothers and a sister and he's healthy. He's mildly autistic so from that standpoint, we've been blessed.

here is the realization that I'm going to have a certain amount of arthritis in my knees. Even one of my fingers, which I jammed pretty badly, is never going to be the same. I know my Achilles, which I injured in 1993, is going to become a factor later in life. There is that reality.

But you understand the risk and you know those things are just a part of playing the game. I don't ever want it to get so bad that I can't walk. Then again, to a certain extent I'm betting on science. I know my knees will need more surgery sooner rather than later, but I'm confident that by the time the pain or lack of mobility becomes a real factor, the medical community will have come up with something.

Every player in the National Football League knows if they play a certain amount of time, parts of their bodies will be messed up. The fingers and hands of offensive linemen, for example; many of those guys have fingers pointing every which way.

It's just the price you pay for working in this industry. We all understand the risks, but we also realize the rewards that can come from taking those risks. And except for those rare situations, the rewards are in line with the price we pay. I'm not so sure my grandfather could have said that about working in the steel mill back in Pittsburgh.

I DON'T KNOW HOW MUCH TIME I HAVE LEFT, BUT I KNOW I'M NOT DONE. WOULD I EVER STICK AROUND TO BE A BACKUP? I DON'T KNOW. BUT I DO KNOW I LOVE THE GAME AND THE COMPETITION. AND I KNOW THERE'S STILL A LOT I'D LIKE TO DO ON THE FOOTBALL FIELD.